ESCHATOLOGY
Truth and Lies:
A Biblical Study

PAUL S. BARRETT

Eschatology Truth and Lies:
A Biblical Study

Bible Study by Paul S. Barrett
Refined version 30

October 2025

Dovetail Publishing
ISBN 978-1-7643546-7-7

Table of Contents

Preface 4
Why is it so important to know and study the End Times? 6
   Who are the signs for? 7
   Where does the word Eschatology come from? 7
   Could God change His mind? 7
End times authors - when did they record their prophecies? 8
What are the 70 weeks of Daniel? 10
Eschatological (End Times) Interpretations 12
Prophetic Signs before His Return 15
Original Scripture Language & Key Translated Definitions 16
   When a word has more than one meaning 19
Biblical Timeline of the Final 7 years before Christ's Millennial Reign 21
Jesus returns as He left 28
Day of The Lord 28
The Book of Revelation Explained 29
   The Structure of the Book of Revelation 31
The 7 seals 34
The 144,000 39
What if One of These Interpretations Is Wrong? 41
   The Danger of False Teaching 42
   Leaders Are Held More Accountable 43
   Could Pre-Tribulation Teaching Lead to Apostasy? 44
Pre-tribulation teaching - truth or deception? 45
When will the mark of the beast be introduced? 47
   Will the mark be mandated or forced? 47
Rapture vs Second Coming 48
What is the Scroll as mentioned in Revelation 5? 49
What Happens After Rapture 50
   The 7 Trumpets 50
   The 7 Bowl Judgements 51
Summary 52
Glossary of Terms 63
   English / Theological Terms 63
   Hebrew Terms (Old Testament) 64
   Greek Terms (New Testament) 65
Scripture Reference Index by Topic/Keyword 66
   Fulfilled & Future Prophesy 66
   False Teachers & Leadership Warnings 66
   Apostasy: Falling Away 66
   Antichrist revealed 66
   Great Tribulation, Persecution 66
   Signs & Celestial Disturbances 67
   Rapture 67
   Second Coming 67
   Day of the Lord 67
   Wrath of God 67

Preface

"My brethren, let not many of you become teachers, knowing that we shall receive a stricter judgment." - **James 3:1**.

From the outset, I want to encourage you to test and research everything. Don't believe everything you hear, even from the pulpit. Learn scripture for yourself.

As a naive Christian, I embraced the teaching that scripture pointed to an imminent rapture. Some ministers in services I attended had specific dates set that came and went. Corrections to these 'calculations' always had an excuse, such as that Roman numerals did not have a zero for the year Jesus was born. But those dates also came and went, by which time I was already skeptical.

Some people believe in a specific eschatological view, sometimes out of fear, but also because they don't think they would survive great tribulation for age/ physical/ medical reasons. Some believe that God wouldn't put His people through such hardships and refuse to consider that this may be a time of testing (perhaps causing a great falling away from God). Another group of Christians come about their view because of the need to align with a particular belief.

I find so many Christians have never been taught about the end times in the church they attend. Their pastors don't preach on sin or end times because they count their success by the size of their congregation, and by preaching on sin or on a topic they see as divisive, or they don't understand, they risk losing numbers in their congregation.

Most pre-tribulation and imminent rapture sermons are preached in a standard 45 to 60-minute Sunday sermon window; usually, selective scriptures are used, and lots of opinions are declared to quell doubt. You cannot possibly teach or summarize End Times theology (approximately 30% of the Bible) in a single 60-minute sermon. It is important to note that imminent rapture taught within the confines of the pre-tribulation rapture theory is relatively new teaching, founded in the last 200 years (made popular by John Darby).

When I revisited the Bible in my 30s, I began to understand that many things taught in entertainment-style churches are not scriptural. I so wanted pre-tribulation rapture to be true especially now that I am a parent - I don't want my kids to see what so many have endured over the last 2000 years; however once I delved into the complexity of the subject, I not only discovered that there are prophesied events that must take place before the 'rapture', I realized that if I was to continue to believe what I had been taught, I was calling Jesus a liar and not believing his own words in **Matthew 24**. I arrived at this discovery by researching many English translations of the Bible (as some omit specific verses entirely), but also by examining the scriptures in the original language. **Matthew, 1 Thessalonians** and **2 Thessalonians,** and **Revelation** were all written in koine (common) Greek, not Latin, as some will suggest. **Joel** and **Malachi** were written in Hebrew, with **Daniel** being written partially in Hebrew and the remainder in Aramaic.

I felt God tell me I had to tell others what I have learned, because of this verse in **Ezekiel 33:6** "*But if the watchman sees the sword coming and does not blow the trumpet to warn the people and the sword comes and takes someone's life, that person's life will be taken because of their sin, but I will hold the watchman accountable for their blood.*"

To understand end times prophecy, I have referenced over 250 verses of scripture, as opposed to other eschatological points of view, where verses are either cherry-picked and misrepresented to mean something that the scripture does not mean at all, or omitted entirely. It is so important to read scripture in context, remembering that chapters were not introduced to the Bible until 1227 AD and verses were not introduced to the Old Testament (the **Hebrew Tanakh**) until 1448 AD, and the New Testament in 1551 AD.

Within this study, I have deliberately separated out non-scriptural 'speculation', often asked as questions, that the Bible does not have specific answers to. My best-guess answers, based on logic and discernment, are contained within FAQ Part 1 and FAQ Part 2. With everything else, I have sourced and referenced Bible passages.

To test what I had been taught and for eschatological events to make chronological sense to me, I decided to write down my learnings, which brought about this document. I have tried to be as thorough as possible; however, I have not included screenshots from the actual Papari from AD50 to AD250, which confirm the authenticity of the scriptures that were written in Greek, as this document would require an additional 120 pages; instead, I intend to share (not teach) what I have learned directly from the Bible.

Why is it so important to know and study the End Times?

- Confidence in what you believe - you should be bold in your knowledge of scripture, and not ignorant.
- So that nobody deceives you - "See to it that no one takes you captive through hollow and deceptive philosophy" (**Colossians 2:8**).
- To see the signs when they eventually occur (**Luke 21:25-28**), and to be prepared
    - Spiritually (is your heart right with God?)
    - Physical preparations - what happens if those alive cannot buy and sell?
    - Mentally - these passages are a warning - to whom? To those who read the Word!
- To give yourself enough time to prepare
- To be able to educate others - and to challenge false beliefs
- To be able to save others, which is our Great Commission (**Matthew 28:19**).

Who are the signs for?

Clearly, those who are reading the Word of God! It is the wise virgins who are taken. The wise virgins were those prepared with enough oil for when the bridegroom arrived (**Matthew 25**).

Where does the word Eschatology come from?

John 6:39-40 uses the Greek word ἔσχατος (***eschatos***) 'last' - "*I will raise them up at the last day.*" **-logia** is the Greek word used for 'study of'. The suffix **-logia** comes from logos which means 'word'.

Could God change His mind?

The Bible has evidence of God changing His mind about carrying out His judgment in the form of destruction and death; however, this only appears to happen when He speaks to individuals - such as Moses in **Exodus 32:1-14** and Jonah in **Jonah 3:1-10**.

We have many prophesied events within scripture that have yet to be fulfilled.

The fact that God has provided insight into the end times, and more importantly, His Son's second coming to so many prophets, and has not agreed to rescind those promises, tells me that He will not change His mind. Prophesied events have always been fulfilled in the Bible without fail. We have no reason to believe that eschatological prophecies will not be fulfilled at some point in the future.

End times authors - when did they record their prophecies?

Daniel was born in Jerusalem around 620 BC, taken into exile in Babylon in 605 BC where he served in Nebuchadnezzar's court, and after Babylon fell to Persia in 539 BC he served under Darius the Mede and Cyrus of Persia. Daniel died somewhere around 530 to 535 BC. **Daniel 9** (the 70 weeks prophesy) was written when Daniel was around 80-85 years old.

Jesus lived ~4 BC to ~AD 30. The Olivet Discourse was recorded shortly before his crucifixion by three of Jesus' disciples in **Matthew 24**, **Mark 13**, and **Luke 21:5-36**. Jesus refers to Daniel's prophesy (**Matthew 24:15**).

Paul, originally named **Saul**, was born in Tarsus between AD 5 and AD 10. A Jew by birth, he became a Pharisee and was trained under the respected teacher Gamaliel (**Acts 22:3**). In his early life as Saul, he zealously persecuted the fledgling church, even participating in the stoning of Stephen (**Acts 7:55-60**; **Acts 8:1-3**). Later, Paul himself reflected on his former life devoted to opposing Christ (**Galatians 1:13**).

There is no scripture that suggests that Saul ever met Jesus in the flesh.

On the road to Damascus, Saul had a supernatural encounter with Jesus and converted to Christianity as recorded in **Acts 9** and recounted in **Acts 22:6-16**. This occurred between 1 and 3 years after Jesus ascended to heaven.

Paul then conducted missionary journeys, including an extended time in Ephesus. He met John, Peter, and James (**Galatians 2:9**). He was imprisoned and later martyred in Rome around AD 64-67 under Nero.

1 Thessalonians and **2 Thessalonians** were written around AD 50-52 during Paul's second missionary journey in Corinth (**Acts 18**) when he was around 40 to 45 years old.

John the Apostle, one of the Twelve Disciples, was present during Jesus' ministry and Olivet Discourse (John, Peter, James, and Andrew all asked Jesus questions that led to the Olivet Discourse). After Jesus' crucifixion and ascension to heaven, John was a respected leader in the church in Jerusalem (**Acts** and **Galatians 2:9**) from around AD 30. In later years, he ministered in Ephesus and Asia; he wrote **1 John**, **2 John**, and **3 John**. John's exile on the island of Patmos during the reign of Emperor Domitian who ruled from AD 81-96. While exiled on the island of Patmos, he wrote the book of **Revelation,** estimated to be around AD 92 to 94.

What are the 70 weeks of Daniel?

The **70 weeks of Daniel** are described in **Daniel 9:24-27**, where the angel Gabriel tells Daniel that "seventy weeks" (literally *seventy sevens* - the Hebrew word "**shavuim**" translates to "sevens") are determined for Israel to fulfill God's redemptive plan.

One "week" equals seven years, if according to **Daniel 7:25** and **Revelation 12:14** where "time, times, and half a time" is 3.5 years. A day is portrayed as a year in **Numbers 14:34** - *"For forty years - one year for each of the forty days you explored the land"* and in **Ezekiel 4:6** - *"I have assigned you 40 days, a day for each year."*

70 × 7 = **490 years** total.

The 70 weeks are divided into:
- 7 weeks (49 years)
- 62 weeks (434 years)
- 1 final week (7 years)

The first 69 weeks:
- *"From the going forth of the command to restore and build Jerusalem"* (**Daniel 9:25**).
    - Dated around 445 BC (Artaxerxes' decree, found in **Nehemiah 2:1-8**).

The first 69 weeks are broken into;

7 Weeks (7x7 = 49 years):
- The time it took to rebuild Jerusalem and its streets and walls (**Nehemiah**, **Ezra**).

62 Weeks (62x7 = 434 years):
- The time from the rebuilding of the temple to *"the coming of the Anointed One"*: Jesus' triumphal entry - **Matthew 21:1-11**, fulfilling **Zechariah 9:9** prophecy (~AD 32)

Total of 69 weeks = 483 years
- From ~ 445 BC to ~ AD 32 matches the 483-year time span when accounting for prophetic years (the Hebrew and Babylonian Calendar was a 354-day year, the Egyptian calendar was a 360-day year). The 69th week ends with Jesus' ascension to heaven.

Dispensationalist Christians often refer to the gap between the 69th and 70th week of Daniel's prophecy as the Church Age.
- The temple was destroyed in 70 AD - fulfilling Jesus' prophecy, during the Church era.
- On May 14, 1948, Israel was reinstated as a nation, fulfilling scriptural 'dry bones' prophecy after spending nearly 2000 years in exile. *"Then he said unto me, Son of man, these bones are the whole house of Israel: behold, they say, Our bones are dried, and our hope is lost: we are cut off for our parts. Therefore, prophesy and say unto them, Thus saith the Lord GOD; Behold, O my people, I will open your graves, and cause you to come up out of your graves, and bring you into the land of Israel."* **Ezekiel 37:11-12**.

This proves that God works with both Israel and the church at the same time. One argument that pre-tribulationists believe is that God doesn't work with the church and with Israel at the same time; they state that God's intention must be to remove the church before He deals again with Israel.

The 70th week
"He [the Antichrist] will confirm a covenant with many for one week. But in the middle of the week, he will put an end to sacrifice and offering" (**Daniel 9:27**).

It is important to note that the term "Daniel's 70th week" is **not** found in the bible. It does refer to the events within the final 7 years before God's judgement.

Eschatological (End Times) Interpretations

Six eschatological interpretations are held within Christianity regarding the timing of the rapture and the experience of believers during end-time events. Each view differs significantly in how it interprets biblical prophecy - particularly the events within the book of Revelation – as well as what defines tribulation, God's wrath, and Christ's return. Understanding these differences is important, as they influence the order of prophetic timelines and form the basis of how believers interpret suffering, divine protection, and spiritual and physical preparedness.

View	Rapture Timing	Believers Experience
Preterism	Believe that the rapture is not Biblical; the belief is that most or all of **Revelation** has already occurred. Events were fulfilled in the 1st century (esp. AD 70 with the fall of Jerusalem)	Nothing. Believers hold the view that **Revelation 2 and Revelation 3** were written specifically to the church in Philadelphia.
Imminence **	At any time.	No prophetic events need to occur. Absolutely won't see 'God's Wrath'. Do not acknowledge the difference between tribulation and wrath.
Pre-tribulation (Pre-trib) **	Before 'tribulation'	Won't be present for 'tribulation', with a focus on 'keep you from the day of trial'. Interprets tribulation as 7 years. ##
Mid-tribulation (Mid-trib)	3.5 years into 'tribulation'	Present for first 3.5 years only. Raptured before bowls.
Pre-wrath	After the first 6 seals are opened (before the 7th seal is opened), therefore before God's wrath (bowl judgements)	Will see the first 6 seals (tribulation), but not the bowl judgements (wrath of God). Acknowledgment that prophetic events must occur before 'rapture' sometime after the midpoint.
Post-tribulation (Post-trib)	End of the 'tribulation period'	The entire tribulation includes the seals and bowls. Will be spiritually protected during this time.

** Most pre-tribulation believers also believe in Imminence. The difference being, is that some pre-tribulation believers who don't believe in imminence believe that the entire 7-year period is God's wrath and will cite **1 Thessalonians 5:9** in isolation.

Some believe in a pre-tribulation rapture without the concept of imminence, believe that Jesus' return will occur once one particular scripture has been fulfilled: *"And this gospel of the kingdom will be preached in all the world as a witness to all the nations, and then the end will come."* - **Matthew 24:14**.

Mid-tribulation and post-tribulation believers often use the same arguments and scriptures cited by the Pre-Wrath view but make assumptions that some words have meanings other than what the original language intended. This may stem from a lack of in-depth study or a full grasp of the topic's complexity, especially given that end-times prophecy and related scriptures account for approximately 30% of the Bible.

Nowhere in the Bible does it refer to the last 7 years as the 'tribulation period'. Note that 3 of the end-times views use the word tribulation to describe their eschatological view. Tribulation has occurred for over 2000 years now - **2 Timothy 3:12** lets us know this will happen - *"all who desire to live godly in Christ Jesus will suffer persecution"*. So, what does the Bible call this period?

The Bible <u>does not</u> refer to these 7 years as "Daniel's 70th week," however, many Christians will cite this description regardless of their view on when the rapture occurs. The Bible <u>does</u> say, in **Daniel 9:27**: *"And he shall confirm the covenant with many for one week: and in the midst of the week he shall cause the sacrifice and the oblation to cease"*.

Prophetic Signs before His Return

What does Jesus say when asked about the signs that His return is coming, in **Matthew 24**? *"What will be the sign of your coming, and of the end of the age?"* (**Matthew 24:3**):

1. First, the Beginning of Sorrows - triggered by the first seal (**Matthew 24:8**).
2. At the midpoint, the antichrist proclaims himself to be god (**2 Thessalonians 2:4**, **Daniel 9:27**).
    a. Great tribulation (**Matthew 24:15**).
    b. The great tribulation is cut short by the celestial signs (**Matthew 24:29**, **Joel 2:31**, **Revelation 6:12-17**), followed by the rapture (God's people are exempt from wrath - **1 Thessalonians 5:9**).
3. The coming of the Son of Man (**Matthew 24:30-31**).

After which time, the 7th seal is broken, which means the scroll can be opened; God's wrath can now be released (starting at **Revelation 8:7**).

Original Scripture Language & Key Translated Definitions

Rapture. *The word 'Rapiemur' is a Latin word used to translate* **harpázō** *(meaning 'caught up' from Greek to Latin; the word 'rapture' is not found in the Bible.* The word '**harpázō**' is the Greek word that translates to 'to be snatched away suddenly' and is used several times in the Bible when outlining eschatological events. It is important to understand that many of the **New Testament** scriptures listed within this paper were **first written in Greek, not Latin.**

The word 'rapture' first appeared in the English language in the 1600s to describe an intense feeling of joy or being carried away emotionally or spiritually. The theological use of the word "Rapture", referring specifically to the event described in **1 Thessalonians 4:17**, became more common in the 18th-19th centuries, especially with the rise of Premillennialism and Dispensationalism in Protestant theology. The Oxford English Dictionary records "Rapture" being used in the religious sense by at least the 17th century, but it became a popular term for eschatological (end-times) events in the 1800s, particularly due to theologians like John Nelson Darby (1800-1882).

The Greek word '**apostasia**' comes from the root word 'apostates', meaning 'rebel' or 'deserter'. English translations of the word '**apostasia**' use 3 different words depending on the version: KJV and NKJV use "Falling away", the NIV and ESV use "Rebellion", while the NASB and CSB translations use the word "Apostasy". The context of **2 Thessalonians 2:3,** regardless of the version, suggests a great departure from the faith will occur before the arrival of the "man of sin" (the Antichrist). "Falling away" does not imply a permanent and sudden removal (**harpázō**). **Harpázō** is a physical removal.

The words 'imminent' and 'imminence' are never used in the Bible. Neither is the term 'tribulation saints'. Be wary of theological terms that are invented to capture your imagination, or become a distraction from actual text.

It is important to **NEVER** use verses to mean what you **WANT** them to mean. There are many verses used to 'suggest' rapture by pre-tribulation teachers. However, if the scripture intended to say rapture, the word 'rapture' (**harpázō**) would have been used.

The Greek word **'Peirasmos'** translates to 'trial', 'to test', and 'temptation'. **Not wrath. Matthew 6:13** we know well.

The Greek word used for **wrath** is '**thymos**' in **Revelation 14:10, Revelation 19:15,** and **Revelation 16:1**, where it refers to the outpouring of God's furious anger. The Bible also uses the Greek word '**orgē**', which also means wrath, in **Romans 2:5, 1 Thessalonians 5:9, and Revelation 6:16-17**.

The Greek word **'thlipsis'**, meaning "**tribulation**/ affliction/ distress", is used in the book of Revelation, and by Jesus in *Matthew 24:21, Matthew 24:9,* and *Matthew 24:29*. The word is also used in **2 Thessalonians 1:4** with regards to persevering *"persecutions and tribulations"*. NOT ONCE DOES TRIBULATION TRANSLATE TO GOD'S WRATH! Tribulation is the suffering at the hands of the prince/ ruler of this world: Satan. Refer to Jesus' own words in **John 14:30**.

The phrase "**tēreō ek**" (τηρέω ἐκ) is used to describe being **kept from** a time of <u>tribulation</u>; *"Because you have kept My command to persevere, I also will <u>**keep you**</u> (**tēreō ek**) from the hour of trial which shall come upon the whole world, to test those who dwell on the earth."* **Revelation 3:10**. Meanwhile, the Greek word "**harpázō**" (ἁρπάζω), meaning 'to seize or snatch away,' is used in **1 Thessalonians 4:17** to describe the catching up of believers; *"Then we who are alive and remain shall be <u>**caught up**</u> (**harpázō**) together with them in the clouds to meet the Lord in the air. And thus, we shall always be with the Lord."* We MUST read this in context with the whole chapter for prophetic events that precede the rapture. Clearly, 'keep from' <u>does not</u> mean rapture.

The phrase *"the blessed hope"* appears only once in Scripture, in **Titus 2:13**, where Paul defines it plainly as *"the appearing of the glory of our great God and Savior, Jesus Christ."* The text does not mention timing relative to tribulation, wrath, or the Antichrist, nor does it describe an escape from suffering, be it tribulation or God's wrath. The New Testament identifies the believer's hope as the resurrection, the return of Christ, and the inheritance of glory (**Acts 23:6**; **Romans 8:18-25**; **Colossians 1:5**; **1 Peter 1:3-7**; **1 John 3:2-3**) - never as avoidance of hardship. In fact, hope is consistently framed in the context of suffering, not the removal of or from suffering (**Romans 5:3-5**; **2 Thessalonians 1:4-7**; **Revelation 13:10**; **Revelation 14:12**).

No passage explicitly states - on any occasion - that the blessed hope is a pre-tribulation escape for the church. Pre-tribulationism must therefore infer its timing from silence rather than text, while overlooking explicit statements that the church will face Antichrist persecution (**Matthew 24:9-22**; **Revelation 13:7**; **Daniel 7:21,25**) and that resurrection and gathering occur *"on the last day"* (**John 6:39-40,44,54**) and *"at the last trumpet"* (**1 Corinthians 15:52**; refer also **Matthew 24:31** and **Revelation 11:15**). Biblically, hope is Christ-centered, not comfort-centered; it looks forward to His appearing, His vindication, and His kingdom. Hope is not intended primarily for personal relief (**2 Thessalonians 1:7-10**; **Revelation 19:6-16**).

When the second coming is reframed as chiefly about what believers avoid, rather than about Christ's victory, glory, and rightful reign, the emphasis subtly shifts from Him to us, a shift the apostles never make. Scripture presents the return of Christ as the culmination of God's redemptive plan, the defeat of evil, the resurrection of the dead, and the public exaltation of the Son (**Philippians 2:9-11**; **Revelation 5:9-14**; **Revelation 19:1-7**). The believer's hope is blessed not because it spares suffering, but because it guarantees resurrection, justice, and eternal union with Christ at His appointed time, in His appointed order.

When a word has more than one meaning

ἐκλεκτός (**eklektós**) is used in both the New and Old Testament. It has various meanings, so it is important to understand the context in which it was written. **Eklektós** translates in various scriptures to *elect, chosen, selected, choice, excellent,* and *precious.* Some pre-tribulation preachers will suggest that the word elect only refers to Israel, so it is important to dig deeper into the specific meaning of each usage.

In the first-century Jewish and Christian context, the word "elect" wasn't a vague spiritual word. It carried specific meaning depending on the scripture, to reference either Israel, Jesus, or the wider church, which was made up of Jews and Gentiles.

1. God's Covenant with Israel:

Israel was called "God's elect" in the Old Testament (**Isaiah 45:4**). To Israel, the elect or "my chosen" meant those God had chosen to enter into a covenant with them. *"For Jacob my servant's sake, and Israel mine elect* (**eklektos**), *I have even called thee by thy name"*

2. Messianic prophecy was fulfilled with the first coming of Jesus:

Jesus Himself is called the Chosen One. "To whom coming, as unto a living stone, disallowed indeed of men, but chosen (**eklektos**) of God, and precious," (**1 Peter 2:4**). **Isaiah 42:1** prophesied the coming of Jesus; *"Behold my servant, whom I uphold; mine elect* (**eklektos**), *in whom my soul delighteth; I have put my spirit upon him: he shall bring forth judgement to the Gentiles"*.

3. The Church:

"Put on therefore, as the elect (**eklektos**) *of God, holy and beloved, bowels of mercies, kindness, humbleness of mind, meekness, longsuffering;"* (**Colossians 3:12**). Believers are elected (chosen) in Him.

As we can see, the word has been used for the nation of Israel, Jesus, <u>and</u> all who belong to Christ.

4. End-Times Usage

In **Matthew 24:22-31**, Jesus tells his disciples that God will shorten the period of great tribulation: *"And except those days should be shortened, there should no flesh be saved: but for the elect's* (**eklektos**) *sake those days shall be shortened"* and will gather *"His elect from the four winds."* Here, "elect" refers to believers who are still on earth at the time of His second coming. It clarifies clearly that "no flesh" should be saved - referring to all believers. If the intention was to say Israel, it would have stated Israel.

5. Direct New Testament References to the Church as the Elect

Romans 8:33 *"Who shall bring a charge against God's elect (**eklektos**)? It is God who justifies."* Here, Paul is clearly speaking of the justified in Christ as the Church, which consists of Jews and Gentiles.

1 Peter 1:2 *"To the elect (**eklektois**) according to the foreknowledge of God the Father, through sanctification of the Spirit, for obedience to Jesus Christ:"* Peter writes to mixed congregations, Jews and Gentiles, in Asia Minor (Pontus, Galatia, Cappadocia, Asia, and Bithynia), calling them all "elect".

1 Peter 2:7 "Now to you who believe", **1 Peter 2:9** *"You are a chosen (**eklekton**) race, a royal priesthood, a holy nation"*. Peter takes covenant titles originally applied to Israel (**Exodus 19:6**; **Isaiah 43:20**) and directly applies them to the Church.

Biblical Timeline of the Final 7 years before Christ's Millennial Reign

The Bible very clearly identifies a period of intense Tribulation (7 seals) and a Period of Wrath (trumpets and bowl judgements). Removing the 7th Seal opens the scroll, which triggers the 7 trumpets, and the 7 bowls follow. The period of intense tribulation and God's wrath cannot be the same thing.

Do not read into scripture what you want to read or justify what you have been taught incorrectly in the past.

1. The teaching of Jesus on the end times is recorded by three separate disciples in **Matthew 24, Mark 13, and Luke 21**, known as the "Olivet Discourse" (sermon on the mount).

2. **Daniel 9:27** - sometimes referred to as 'Daniel's 70th week' - is the prophecy that Jesus refers to in **Matthew 24**. The 70th week is 7 years long. At the midpoint, the Abomination of Desolation occurs. 1,260 days later, Christ returns, defeating Antichrist at Armageddon. **Daniel 12:11** adds an extra 30 days, which may represent the cleansing of the temple before the Millennial Kingdom begins (**Daniel 8:14, Ezekiel 43, Zechariah 13:2, Zechariah 14**).

    a. At the Midpoint, the Abomination of Desolation occurs, there will be 1290 days **(Daniel 12:11)**, Armageddon begins **(Revelation 16:16)**. Jesus says in **Matthew 24:15,** *"When you see the abomination of desolation spoken of by the prophet Daniel, standing in the holy place (let the reader understand)."* If the church has already been raptured, as pre-tribulation teachers believe, who will be left on earth to read scripture to understand? The fact is that the rapture hasn't occurred yet because eschatological events must occur first. We are called to look for the signs that the end is near, so we are not deceived, and so we are not living in fear.

3. The specific lengths of time (1,260 days, 42 months, or *"time, times, and half a time"*) appear in **Revelation** and **Daniel** and are often interpreted as 3.5 years. **Daniel 9:27**, which speaks of a final "week" (7 years) with severe events in the last half (3.5 years). When the covenant is made with Israel, the 70th week begins.

4. **2 Thessalonians 2:1-4** clearly states that two things must occur **before** Jesus returns:
   a. First, the falling away happens (apostasia). **Matthew 24:11** also makes this clear.
   b. Second, the *"man of sin"* (antichrist) is revealed (**2 Thessalonians 2:3-4**) - he exalts himself above God and sits in the temple of God. **Matthew 24:15** *"So when you see the abomination of desolation, spoken of by the prophet Daniel* [**Daniel 9:27**], *standing in the holy place."* **Matthew 24:21** *"for then shall be great tribulation"*.
   c. **Matthew 24:29** *"Immediately <u>after</u> the <u>tribulation</u> of those days..."* we will see and experience **Tribulation**, NOT **wrath.**

5. **Matthew 24:9** *"Then you will be handed over to be persecuted and put to death, and you will be hated by all nations because of me."* This warning comes immediately after the "beginning of birth pains" Jesus speaks about in **Matthew 24:8**. In **John 15:18** Jesus tells His disciples that the world will hate them because *"it hated me first"*. In **1 Peter 4:14** believers are told they are blessed if they are insulted or suffer *"because of the name of Christ"*. **Revelation 12:17** - The dragon makes war on *"those who keep God's commands and hold fast their testimony about Jesus."* The persecution described in all these scriptures is directed specifically at those who follow Christ. Only the church suffers hatred because of His name. Israel as a nation is still awaiting the Messiah and is not persecuted "for Jesus' name."

6. **Revelation chapters 6 and 7** clearly state that we will face persecution **before** the rapture in **Revelation 7:14**. The events associated with each of the 7 seals on the scroll are described in **Revelation 5:1**:
    a. The 1st seal is the white horse. False prophets are present. The Antichrist appears (**Revelation 6:1-2**)
    b. The 2nd seal brings wars, no peace, people killing people (**Revelation 6:3-4**).
    c. The 3rd seal is Famine (**Revelation 6:5-6**).
    d. **1 Thessalonians 3:3-4** confirms that tribulation is to be expected, *"that no one should be shaken by these afflictions; for you yourselves know that we are appointed to this. For, in fact, we told you before when we were with you that we would suffer tribulation."*
    e. The 4th seal is pestilence and killing with the sword of God's Elect in large numbers (**Revelation 6:7-8**). How can this possibly be God's wrath on His own people? This is <u>tribulation</u>, as the scriptures state!
    f. The 5th seal is Christian martyrs asking God for justice (**Revelation 6:9-11**).
    The 5th seal proves that the wrath of God and the seals heralding tribulation are two different things. **Revelation 6:10** clearly states, "How long, Sovereign Master, holy and true, before you judge those who live on the earth and **avenge our blood?**". This couldn't be clearer that the eschatological wrath of God has not begun yet.
    g. The 6th seal brings a "great earthquake", the sun turns black, the full moon like blood, and stars of the sky fall to the earth. If you didn't know you were in tribulation before, you certainly do now. **Joel 2:31** states very clearly that *"The sun shall be turned to darkness, and the moon to blood, **before** the great and awesome day of the Lord comes."* Then the kings of the earth, the rich and the powerful, hide in caves. They certainly know now that something isn't right.

The 6 seals in **Revelation** line up perfectly with the teaching of Jesus in **Matthew 24** during His Olivet Discourse.

    h. The 7th seal is the Day of the Lord's Wrath. This is the announcement of the trumpets and bowl judgements. When all 7 seals are removed, the scroll is now opened, and 7 angels with 7 trumpets are introduced. Then one at a time, each angel blows their trumpet: 7 new prophetic events take place. (see pages 51-52)

7. The second half of the 70th week (3.5 years) is what Jesus prophesies as *"Great Tribulation"* in **Matthew 24:21**. For more periods of time defined in this final week, see also
    a. **Revelation 11:2** - The holy city is trampled for 42 months (3.5 years).
    b. **Revelation 11:3** - The two witnesses prophesy for 1,260 days (3.5 years).
    c. **Revelation 13:5** - The Beast (Antichrist) rules for 42 months (3.5 years).

8. We are not called to live in fear of what the end times may bring, but we are to **look for the signs**. **Luke 21:25-28** *"There will be signs in the sun and moon and stars…. They will see the Son of Man coming in a cloud with power and great glory. Now when these things begin to take place, straighten up and raise your heads, because **your** redemption is drawing near."*

9. **Matthew 24:22** Jesus is speaking about the Great Tribulation: *"but for the elect's sake those days shall be shortened"*.
    a. **Matthew 24:29** says, *"Immediately AFTER the tribulation of those days"* we will see celestial signs: *"the sun be darkened, and the moon shall not give her light, and the stars shall fall from heaven"*. If Christians around the globe see these signs, the signs must be blatantly obvious, probably striking fear into the hearts of those not prepared to 'see the signs'.

Jesus returns, and the rapture occurs... On the same day. Jesus states this will be as with Noah: Noah entered the ark, and the rain began on the same day. Similarly, Lot left Sodom, and judgment came on the same day - **Luke 17:28-30** *"on the day"* (singular day). Nowhere does Jesus say that the "day of the Lord" is 7 years long or any longer than one day. The "day of the Lord" is not the whole tribulation and wrath periods. The "day of the Lord" occurs at the 7th seal. **Luke 17:30** *"Even so it will be in the day when the Son of Man is revealed."*

10. The celestial signs of the 6th seal indicate that God's wrath is **about** to begin.
    a. **Joel 2:31** states very clearly that *"The sun shall be turned to darkness, and the moon to blood, **before** the great and awesome day of the Lord comes."* These are celestial signs that are prophesied to occur **before** Jesus returns.

11. Without using the word rapture, we are told that *"The Lord himself will descend from heaven with a cry of command, with the voice of an archangel, and with the sound of the trumpet of God. And the dead in Christ will rise first. Then we who are alive, who are left, will be caught up* (**harpázō**) *together with them in the clouds to meet the Lord in the air, and so we will always be with the Lord."* (**1 Thessalonians 4:16-17**). **Matthew 24:30-31** parallels this.

12. **1 Thessalonians 4:16-18** speaks to the details of the 'rapture'; **1 Thessalonians 4:17** *"Then we who are alive and remain shall be caught up* (**harpázō**) *together with them* (the dead in Christ from **1 Thessalonians 4:16**) *in the clouds to meet the Lord in the air"*.

13. Paul says in
    a. **1 Thessalonians 1:10** "*and to wait for His Son from heaven, whom He raised from the dead - Jesus, who delivers us from the wrath (**orgē**) to come.*"
    b. **1 Thessalonians 5:9** "*For God has not appointed us to wrath (**orgē**), but to obtain salvation through our Lord Jesus Christ.*"
    c. **Romans 5:9** "*Much more then, having now been justified by His blood, we shall be saved from wrath (**orgē**) through Him.*"
    d. John writes in **Revelation 3:10,** "*Because you have kept My command to persevere, I also will **keep you** (tēreō ek) from the hour of trial which shall come upon the whole world, to test those who dwell on the earth.*" To 'keep from' does not mean permanent 'removal from'.

14. **Malachi 4:5** "*Behold, I will send you Elijah the prophet <u>before</u> the coming of the great and dreadful day of the Lord.*"

15. **Revelation 6:12-17** - The *sixth seal* opens, causing a great earthquake, cosmic disturbances, and people hide themselves. **Revelation 6:17** "*For the great day of His **wrath** (orgē) <u>has come</u>, and who is able to stand?*"
    Revelation 7:9-17 - A multitude of those who have "*come out of the great tribulation*" (**Revelation 7:14**) from all nations are seen before God's throne, praising Him and receiving protection from suffering.
    Revelation 8-9 - The *seventh seal* is opened, leading to the trumpet judgments, including hail, fire, locusts, and plagues, causing widespread destruction and suffering. See **page 51** for more details on the trumpet judgements.
    Revelation 16 - The Bowl Judgements. See **page 52** for more details on the bowl judgements.

16. After the *celestial signs* in **Revelation 6:12-17,** we are told in **Revelation 7:2** that an angel will declare a command: *"Do not harm the earth or the sea or the trees until we have sealed the servants of our God on their foreheads"*. 12,000 from each tribe (144,000) are sealed to protect them from the wrath that is to come… they are the witnesses to the judgment about to begin. According to **Revelation 7,** this occurs BEFORE the explanation of who these people are in **Revelation 7:14**;
    a. Directly after the 144,000 are sealed, **Revelation 7:9-17** states that a great multitude was standing before the throne: *"These are the ones coming **out of** the great tribulation…"* (**Revelation 7:14**).

17. **2 Peter 3:11-12** *"waiting for and hastening the coming of the day of God… the heavens will be set on fire and dissolved, and the heavenly bodies will melt as they burn."*

18. The rapture triggers the day of the Lord on the same day. **1 Thessalonians 5:4-9 & 2 Thessalonians 1:6-10** - the righteous are rescued.

19. Wrath is described in **Revelation 16:1:** *"Then I heard a loud voice from the temple saying to the seven angels, 'Go and pour out the bowls of the wrath of God on the earth.'"*

20. The 5th trumpet judgement is 5 months long: refer to **Revelation 9:1 and Revelation 9:5**. Note that the trumpet judgements occur **after** the seals, so any (post-tribulation) date setting for a rapture is irrelevant (remembering that the 'rapture' occurs after the 6th seal is opened).

Jesus returns as He left

Acts 1:9-11 *"... a cloud received Him out of their sight... This same Jesus, who was taken up from you into heaven, will so come in like manner as you saw Him go in to heaven."* This passage ties Jesus' ascension in a cloud to His future return in the same manner - **Revelation 1:7**.

"The Lord himself will descend from heaven with a cry of command, with the voice of an archangel, and with the sound of the trumpet of God. And the dead in Christ will rise first. Then we who are alive, who are left, will be **caught up** (**harpázō**) *together with them in the clouds to meet the Lord in the air, and so we will always be with the Lord."* (**1 Thessalonians 4:16-17**).

Revelation 20:4-6 states, *"Blessed and holy is he that hath part in the first resurrection; on such the second death hath no power, but they shall be priests of God and of Christ, and shall reign with Him a thousand years."*

Day of The Lord

Obadiah 1:15 *"For the day of the Lord is near upon all heathen* (**gôy**); *as thou hast done, it shall be done unto you."* **Gôy** also translates from Hebrew to English as 'nations' or 'gentiles', meaning 'non-Hebrew people'

The Book of Revelation Explained

The book of Revelation is written to record a series of visions that John the apostle is shown. Some of these visions move forward in order sequentially, while others pause the story to explain what is happening behind the scenes. **Revelation** gives clues when events are moving forward, using phrases like "after these things" (**Revelation 4:1; 7:1; 15:5**). The seven seals in **Revelation 6** clearly unfold one after another, and the seventh seal leads directly into the seven trumpets (**Revelation 8:1-2**), showing that these judgments are connected and progressing. In the same way, the seventh trumpet (**Revelation 11:15-19**) does not signify an end to anything but opens the way to provide detail about the next series of events, being the seven bowls, which are clearly described as the wrath of God (**Revelation 15:1; 16:1**). There is a clear distinction between earlier suffering caused by mankind and by Satan, and later judgment that comes directly from God.

At several points, **Revelation** stops the forward movement of events to give explanation and clarity. These sections do not advance the timeline but instead add understanding. Examples include **Revelation 7**, which explains the sealing of the 144,000 and the great multitude who have just come out of the great tribulation; **Revelation 10-11**, which focuses on the two witnesses; and **Revelation 12-14**, which explains the spiritual battle behind persecution on earth. These passages mirror earlier scriptures within the Bible. **Revelation 12** reflects the same conflict and time period found in **Daniel 7** and **Daniel 12:1-7**, using the same time description of "time, times, and half a time." **Revelation 11** draws from **Zechariah 4** in its description of the two witnesses, and **Revelation 13** clearly builds on **Daniel 7** when describing the final world empire. This shows that Revelation is explaining and completing earlier prophecies, not changing them nor is the book creating new prophecies.

Revelation brings together what God has already revealed through the prophets and through Jesus Himself. Events such as the cosmic signs (**Revelation 6:12-17** mirrors **Joel 2:30-31** and Jesus' own words in **Matthew 24:29**), the events listed to occur when the Day of the Lord begins (**Revelation 8-16** mirrors **Isaiah 13** and **Zephaniah 1**), and the resurrection of the unbelieving dead and the final judgement (**Revelation 20:5** and **Revelation 20:12-13** mirrors **Daniel 12:2**) all show the same pattern taught elsewhere in Scripture. **Revelation** does not stand alone, but ties everything together, showing how and when these events unfold.

Reading Revelation correctly means recognizing when the text is moving forward in time and when it is pausing to explain backstories, allowing Scripture to interpret Scripture rather than forcing Revelation into a single straight-line timeline.

The Structure of the Book of Revelation

Revelation Section	Scripture	Purpose	Revelation Timeline Function	Old / New Testament Parallel or foreshadowing
Letters to the Churches	Revelation 1:1-3:22	Establishes the spiritual condition believers need to be in before end-time events	Background	Matthew 24:4-14
Throne Room in Heaven	Revelation 4-5	Reveals God's authority before judgment begins	Background	Isaiah 6:1-5; Daniel 7:9-14
Beginning of Sorrows	Daniel 12:4	Warning to look for the signs	Prelude	Matthew 24:6-8
Seven Seals	Revelation 6:1-17, Revelation 8:1	Antichrist led deception then tribulation events unfold one after another	Sequential	Matthew 24:9-29; ~~Zechariah 6:1-8~~
Sealing of the 144,000 & Great Multitude	Revelation 7	Explains who is protected before God's wrath	Explanation	Ezekiel 9:3-4; Daniel 12:1
Seven Trumpets	Revelation 8:2-11:19	God's judgments begin	Sequential	Joel 2:1-11
Mighty Angel & Little Book	Revelation 10	Explains delay and remaining prophecy	Explanation	Daniel 12:4-9

Revelation Section	Scripture	Purpose	Revelation Timeline Function	Old / New Testament Parallel or foreshadowing
Two Witnesses	Revelation 11:1-13	Testimony and persecution during tribulation	Set timeframe within timeline	Zechariah 4:1-14; Daniel 12:7
Seventh Trumpet	Revelation 11:15-19	7th Trumpet declares Christ's kingdom and God's wrath	Sequential	Psalm 2; Daniel 7:13-14
Woman, Dragon, and Beasts	Revelation 12-13	Explains spiritual and political forces	Explanation	Genesis 3:15; Daniel 7
Warning and Harvest	Revelation 14	Announces judgment and separation	Transitional	Joel 3:12-14; Matthew 13:37-43
Seven Bowls of Wrath	Revelation 15-16	Final outpouring of God's wrath	Sequential	Isaiah 13:6-13; Zephaniah 1:14-18
Fall of Babylon	Revelation 17-18	Judgment of the world system	Focused explanation	Jeremiah 51; Isaiah 47
Return of Christ	Revelation 19	Christ returns in power and judgment	Sequential	Matthew 24:30; Zechariah 14:3-5
Millennial Reign	Revelation 20:1-6	Satan restrained. Christ 1000-year reign begins	Sequential	Isaiah 2:2-4; Daniel 7:27

Revelation Section	Scripture	Purpose	Revelation Timeline Function	Old / New Testament Parallel or foreshadowing
Final Judgment	Revelation 20:7-15	Resurrection and judgment	Sequential	Daniel 12:2
New Heaven and New Earth	Revelation 21-22	Eternal restoration	Sequential	Isaiah 65:17-25

The 7 seals

There are over 30 parallels between the teaching of Jesus in **Matthew** and the teaching of Paul in **Thessalonians** - the Bible was the first hyperlinked book ever written!

The seven seals, described in **Revelation** chapters **6, 7,** and **8**, represent the opening sequence of events released from the scroll which will be opened by the Lamb (**Revelation 6:1**). Each seal unveils a stage of progression that leads the world closer to the Day of the Lord. These are not yet the outpourings of God's wrath, but rather the beginning of birth pains Jesus spoke of in **Matthew 24:4-8**. They include deception, war, famine, death, martyrdom, and great cosmic disturbances, culminating in silence in heaven before the trumpet judgments are introduced. The seals reveal what must take place before God's wrath begins. They expose human corruption, satanic deception, and global turmoil. The signs Jesus warned of - false christs, wars, famines, and earthquakes - align directly with these early seals.

Old Testament prophets also foresaw these same events: Isaiah (**Isaiah 13:6-13**), Ezekiel (**Ezekiel 30:3**), Joel (**Joel 2:30-31**), Zephaniah (**Zephaniah 1:14-18**), and Malachi (**Malachi 4:5**) describe signs and a time of distress that would precede the great and terrible Day of the Lord. The seals therefore serve both as signs and as divine preparation, marking the transition from human rebellion to divine intervention.

The 7 seals listed in Revelation are mirrored elsewhere in scripture:

Revelation (John)	Event	Mirrored Reference
First Seal (**Revelation 6:1-2**)	False prophets (White horse)	**Matthew 24:4-5**
	The Antichrist is revealed and gains power through false peace - a 7-year covenant is confirmed by the Antichrist.	**Matthew 24:15** **Daniel 9:29**
2nd Seal (**Revelation 6:3-4**)	Wars (Red horse)	**Matthew 24:6-7**
3rd Seal (**Revelation 6:5-6**)	Famine (Black horse)	**Matthew 24:7**
4th Seal (**Revelation 6:7-8**)	Martyrdom, Great Tribulation (Sickly horse)	**Matthew 24:9, Matthew 24:21-22 2 Timothy 3:12**
5th Seal (**Revelation 6:9-11**)	Result of Martyrdom	**Matthew 24:21-22**
6th Seal (**Revelation 6:12-17**)	Celestial Disturbances	**Matthew 24:29 Luke 21:25-26 Joel 2:30-31**
Jesus returns (**Revelation 7:9-17**), those coming out of the great tribulation (**Revelation 7:14**)	Jesus returns, Rapture of Saints	**Matthew 24:30-31**
7th Seal (**Revelation 8:1**) Prelude to wrath (**Revelation 8:2-6**)	Day of the Lord's Wrath	**Matthew 24:30 Matthew 24:37-41**
7 Trumpets Trumpets 1 to 4 (**Revelation 8:7-13**) Trumpets 5 & 6 (**Revelation 9**) 2 Witnesses (**Revelation 11:1-13**) Trumpet 7 (**Revelation 11:15-19**) 7 Bowls (**Revelation 15:7, Revelation 16:1-21**)	Judgement on a wicked earth	**Joel 2:1-11 Isaiah 13:9-13**

Pre-tribulationists who state that Matthew is speaking about Israel and not the church fail to recognize that Matthew is the **only** gospel to include The Great Commission (**Matthew 28:19-20**), Church discipline (**Matthew 18:15-20**), and is the only gospel that mentions the word church (**ekklesia**) (**Matthew 16:18, 18:17**).

When many pre-tribulation preachers interpret Jesus' teaching in **Matthew 24** - applying **Matthew 24:29-31** to mean Armageddon instead of the rapture - they also alter the meaning of the parables that follow. This shift creates inconsistencies, as **Matthew 24:36** and **Matthew 24:44** emphasize the unpredictability of Christ's coming, which would not make sense if they referred to Armageddon; Armageddon is preceded by prophesied events. Since the parables in **Matthew 24** and **Matthew 25** build upon the teaching in **Matthew 24:30-31**, changing their meaning distorts Jesus' intended message about watchfulness and readiness.

Imminent rapture believers need **2 Thessalonians 2:3** to have the word Apostasia mean rapture. However, if rapture was the intention, the word **harpázō** would have been used.

Believing false doctrine will undoubtedly lead Christians to fall away from the faith if they were still present during the first 4 seals of the tribulation. They may even feel like they are 'forced' or have 'no choice' but to take the mark to eat. We don't know with any certainty when the mark of the beast will be introduced.

The Greek word for 'keep' is '**tēreō**'. '**Tēreō ek**' is Greek for 'keep from'. God kept Noah from the effects of the flood, but he still went through the event. God kept Daniel protected in the lion's den, not out of it. God kept Shadrach, Meshach, and Abednego safe from the inferno they were thrown into - they were protected. The same word, '**tēreō**', is used repeatedly in scripture. You cannot use one word to have two different definitions just because you want it to mean what you want it to.

Throughout history, God has kept His people safe. God protected the Israelites who left Egypt; Egyptian secular scrolls suggest that as many as 2 million Israelites left Egypt in Exodus; not all left - the 2 million is estimated to have been 20-40% of the Israelite population at the time. Christians and Jews were persecuted right through history - those who prepared were saved. 5 to 6 million Jews were killed during the holocaust. Many who prepared or saw the signs of what was coming escaped.

Revelation 3:10 "I will keep (**tēreō ek**) you from the hour of trial (not out of; **harpázō** is not used here). **Revelation** was written in Greek. The Greek 'ἐκ' translates to "out of/ keep from/ keep away from"; while '**tēreō**' translates to 'keep/ guard/ protect/ watch over'. This means that Christians are protected from the great tribulation, **not taken out of it**. The *same words* are used in **John 17:15**, where Jesus very specifically says, *"I do not pray that You should take them out of the world but that You should keep them from the evil one"* - not removal (**harpázō**) from the world! We cannot be selective on what Jesus' own words are in both **Matthew 24** and **John 17** - the word '**tēreō**' is used, not '**harpázō**'.

A preacher teaching imminent rapture recently stated that according to **2 Thessalonians 2:3**, the rapture (departure) occurs first, then the man of sin is revealed. However, this contradicts both **Revelation 6:1-17** and Jesus' own words in **Matthew 24**; He warns that when we see the false Christs, these people will "deceive the very elect" (**Matthew 24:24**) - this tells us that God's people will still be on earth! If people are not allowed to buy and sell without the mark, what will the pre-tribulation believers do if they are unprepared?

Matthew 24:29-31 is a prophecy about events that must happen (otherwise you are saying that Jesus is a liar if you suggest that no events must take place) and ends with the promise that the elect (**eklektós**) are gathered.

21. It is important to get the Greek translation correct when reading **Matthew 24:37-41**.

    a. **Matthew 24:39** states, "*and took* **(ἅπαντας, hápantas)** *them all away,*" referring to the ungodly who perished in the Flood.
        i. This parallels those who did not leave Sodom (**Luke 17:28-30**).
    b. **Luke 17:27** and **Luke 17:29** use **pántas**, not **hápantas**, for "*destroyed them all.*" Both words indicate total destruction, but with slightly different emphases.
    c. **Matthew 24:40** – "*One shall be taken* **(paralambanō)** *and the other left.*"
    d. **Matthew 24:41** – "*One shall be taken* **(paralambanō)** *and the other left.*"
    e. **John 14:3** – Jesus says, "*I will come again and take* **(paralambanō)** *you to myself, that where I am, you may be also.*"
    f. The wise virgins were taken, not the unprepared virgins (**Matthew 25:1-13**).

The 144,000

Following the rapture and immediately prior to the outpouring of Gods wrath starting with the trumpet judgements (**Revelation 8-9**), God seals the 144,000 from the twelve tribes of Israel between the sixth and seventh seals (**Revelation 7:1-8**), marking them with His own seal on their foreheads to protect them when judgment is poured out. These 144,000 remain on the earth, not to experience or suffer God's wrath, but as protected witnesses during the Day of the Lord (**Revelation 7:3**, and **Revelation 9:4**). Their sealing occurs in very close timing to the rapture (likely minutes or hours), as **Revelation 7** reveals a great multitude already in heaven who have "*come out of the great tribulation*" immediately after naming the revised list of tribes (**Revelation 7:9-14**), demonstrating that removal and sealing are distinct but sequential acts. Preserved through the trumpet judgments, the 144,000 later reappear alive and victorious with the Lamb on Mount Zion, still bearing "*his Father's name written in their foreheads.*" (**Revelation 14:1**). The 144,000 are not overlooked by the rapture but appointed to remain as witnesses on earth not appointed to wrath (**Revelation 9:4** and **1 Thessalonians 5:9**). In a world now fully aware that the Day of the Lord has arrived (**Joel 2:30-31**), these 144,000 witnesses are living evidence that God distinguishes His own – clearly these cannot be those who took the mark of the beast on their right hand or forehead. They are protected witnesses, similar to Noah before the flood (**Hebrews 11:7**). Their sealing confirms that God will not pour out His wrath without first securing both the removal of the church and protecting those He has chosen to remain.

The 144,000 are sealed as 12,000 from each of twelve tribes of Israel as listed in **Revelation 7**. This list is not identical to the sons of Jacob, with Dan omitted and Joseph included alongside Manasseh (compare **Revelation 7:5-8** with **Genesis 49** and **Numbers 1**). This reflects God's judgment on past sin and idolatry in the tribes, **Judges 18:30-31** records that "*the children of Dan set up the graven* (carved) *image*".

Despite the 10 tribes in the Northern Kingdom (called Israel) being conquered by Assyria in around 722 BC (**2 Kings 17:6**), **Revelation 7** would indicate that God is showing that the sealing of 12,000 from each tribe is based on His knowledge of who and where these people are, not on human records. Even if their lineage is hidden or scattered, God knows who belongs to Him. Scripture states that Israel was scattered among the nations long before Christ and remains dispersed throughout the world (**2 Kings 17:6** and **James 1:1**), and that God gathers and works with His people from "*the four corners of the earth*" (**Isaiah 11:12**, and the rapture of the elect in **Matthew 24:31**). In this context, it is reasonable to understand that the 144,000 could at the time be living all over the world and remain geographically dispersed during the Day of the Lord, to be witnesses on each continent within each nation and city as judgment unfolds worldwide. Their continued presence across the earth testifies that God's wrath is global (**Isaiah 13:9-11**, **Isaiah 24:1-6**, **Isaiah 26:21**, **Matthew 24:21-22**, **Luke 21:35**, **Revelation 8:7-12**), yet His protection is precise, but His seal upon His servants (**Revelation 7:3**) is deliberate and unmistakable.

For those who believe and/or teach that **Isaiah 11:12** was fulfilled in 1948, do not understand that **Isaiah 11** is Messianic prophecy because it describes a coming ruler coming from the line of David.

Ezekiel 37 itself has two parts – first the 'dry bones' are brought together as a national restoration (fulfilled in 1948), and secondly, breath enters the bones, which points to a spiritual restoration – with **Isaiah 11:1** "*a Branch shall grow out of his roots*" describing the Branch from Jesse ruling in righteousness, and a world filled with the knowledge of the LORD (**Isaiah 11:9**).

What if One of These Interpretations Is Wrong?

If **pre-wrath**, **mid-tribulation**, or **post-tribulation** interpretations are incorrect and a **pre-tribulation rapture** is true, all believers will be with Christ when He comes.

However, if prophetic events begin to unfold and believers remain on earth, those who have taught the **pre-tribulation view** will be held accountable for misleading others (**James 3:1; Ezekiel 33:6**). Many Christians could find themselves unprepared - physically, mentally, and spiritually disillusioned because they were expecting to be taken before any tribulation occurred.

If a particular teaching is presented from the pulpit as truth, yet that teaching is incorrect, does it amount to false teaching? Could this be why the first words of Jesus in **Matthew 24:4**, in response to His disciples' question about His return, were, *"Watch out that no one deceives you"*?

The Danger of False Teaching

The Bible warns extensively about false teachers who mislead people with popular but incorrect doctrines:

2 Timothy 4:3-4 *"For the time will come when people will not put up with sound doctrine. Instead, to suit their own desires, they will gather around them a great number of teachers to say what their itching ears want to hear. They will turn their ears away from the truth and turn aside to myths."*

2 Peter 2:1 *"But there were also false prophets among the people, just as there will be false teachers among you. They will secretly introduce destructive heresies, even denying the sovereign Lord who bought them, bringing swift destruction on themselves."*

Matthew 24:11 *"And many false prophets will arise and mislead many."* (Jesus speaking about end times)

Jeremiah 23:16 *"This is what the LORD Almighty says: 'Do not listen to what the prophets are prophesying to you; they fill you with false hopes. They speak visions from their own minds, not from the mouth of the LORD.'"*

Colossians 2:8 *"See to it that no one takes you captive through hollow and deceptive philosophy, which depends on human tradition and the elemental spiritual forces of this world rather than on Christ."*

If believers are not deeply grounded in Bible study or are 'Sunday Christians', they may lack the scriptural knowledge to recognize what is happening. This could lead to confusion, fear, and even apostasy (falling away from the faith).

Leaders Are Held More Accountable

The Bible teaches that those in leadership positions bear a greater responsibility because of their influence over others:

James 3:1 "*Not many of you should become teachers, my fellow believers, because you know that we who teach will be judged more strictly.*"

Ezekiel 33:6 "*But if the watchman sees the sword coming and does not blow the trumpet to warn the people and the sword comes and takes someone's life, that person's life will be taken because of their sin, but I will hold the watchman accountable for their blood.*"

Matthew 18:6 "*If anyone causes one of these little ones - those who believe in me - to stumble, it would be better for them to have a large millstone hung around their neck and to be drowned in the depths of the sea.*"

Acts 20:29-30 "*I know that after I leave, savage wolves will come in among you and will not spare the flock. Even from your own number, men will arise and distort the truth in order to draw away disciples after them.*"

Could Pre-Tribulation Teaching Lead to Apostasy?

With the pre-tribulation rapture theory being a relatively new yet widely accepted doctrine, could it contribute to some believers falling away (the apostasy mentioned in **2 Thessalonians 2:3**)? If believers who expected an early escape instead find themselves tested through suffering, will many fall away from the faith in disappointment, or question Christianity?

2 Thessalonians 2:3 *"Let no one deceive you in any way. For that day will not come, unless* (the Greek word for unless is '**ean mē**') *the rebellion ('***apostasia***') comes first ('***prōton***'), and the man of lawlessness is revealed, the son of destruction."*
Matthew 24:9-10 *"Then they will deliver you up to tribulation and put you to death, and you will be hated by all nations for my name's sake. And then many will fall away and betray one another and hate one another."*
Revelation 13:10 *"If anyone is to be taken captive, to captivity he goes; if anyone is to be slain with the sword, with the sword must he be slain. Here is a call for the endurance and faith of the saints."*

Whether you hold to a **Pre-Tribulation, Mid-Tribulation, Post-Tribulation**, or **Pre-Wrath** point of view, believers must be spiritually prepared for testing (**Matthew 24:13; Revelation 14:12**). If tribulation comes and believers are still on earth, those who have been taught a pre-tribulation rapture and do not have a deeper biblical understanding may be caught off guard, unprepared, and will potentially lose faith (**Luke 8:13**).

Pre-tribulation teaching - truth or deception?

Imminent rapture is a new concept, only coming into the theological discussion around 1830 AD. However, there are 5 precursors listed in scriptures that occur **before** the rapture. (**Matthew 24**);

    a. "Birth Pains" - **Matthew 24:7-8** *"For nation shall rise against nation, and kingdom against kingdom: and there shall be famines, and pestilences, and earthquakes, in diverse places. All these are the beginning of sorrows."*

    b. Falling Away (apostasy) - **1 Timothy 4:1, 2 Thessalonians 2:3, Matthew 24:10-12** - *"And then many will be offended, will betray one another, and will hate one another. Then, many false prophets will rise up and deceive many. And because lawlessness will abound, the love of many will grow cold.";* ***2 Timothy 4:3-4*** *- "For the time will come when they will not endure sound doctrine, but according to their own desires, because they have itching ears, they will heap up for themselves teachers; and they will turn their ears away from the truth, and be turned aside to fables."*

    c. Abomination of Desolation - **Daniel 9:27, Daniel 11:31, Daniel 12:11, 2 Thessalonians 2:3-4, Matthew 24:15-16** *"Therefore, when you see the 'abomination of desolation,' spoken of by Daniel the prophet, standing in the holy place (whoever reads, let him understand), then let those who are in Judea flee to the mountains."*

    d. Unparalleled Persecution of Christians - **2 Timothy 3:12, Revelation 6:9-11, Revelation 13:7** – *"It was granted to him to make war with the saints and to overcome them. And authority was given him over every tribe, tongue, and nation."* (not just Israel); **Matthew 24:9-10** – *"Then they will deliver you up to tribulation and kill you, and you will be hated by all nations for My name's sake. And then*

> many will be offended, will betray one another, and will hate one another."

e. Multi-faceted Celestial Disturbance - **Luke 21:25-26, Joel 2:30-31, Matthew 24:29, Revelation 6:12-14** – *"I looked when He opened the sixth seal, and behold, there was a great earthquake; and the sun became black as sackcloth of hair, and the moon became like blood. And the stars of heaven fell to the earth, as a fig tree drops its late figs when it is shaken by a mighty wind. Then the sky receded as a scroll when it is rolled up, and every mountain and island was moved out of its place."*

These clearly prophesy that defined events must occur before a rapture can occur.

In speaking to so many Christians who believe in a pre-tribulation (or imminent) rapture, I discovered that not a single one of them came to their position on the rapture by reading only the Bible – because the evidence for this position simply isn't there. These believers came to this position based on the teachings, or videos, or books of others, not on the scripture itself.

When will the mark of the beast be introduced?

The timing of this prophesied event (**Revelation 13:16-18**) is unclear. We can look for the signs and speculate that it could be around the time of the 3rd seal (**Matthew 24:7**, **Revelation 6:5-6**). If there is widespread famine, what better time to introduce a system whereby *"no man can buy or sell"* - followed by a time of intense hatred and *"Great Tribulation"* (**Matthew 24:21**) where those who do not submit to the beast system experience hardships like never before.

Will the mark be mandated or forced?

Revelation 14:9-11 tells us that those who receive the mark will worship the beast. It will likely be a conscious act to receive the mark. It will be tied to a global economic cashless system, whereby those without the mark cannot buy and sell. The Bible does not state what the mark is - speculation suggests that it could be a tattoo, microchip, nano technology injection/implant, or a digital ID. The spiritual and symbolic implications are that it could control thoughts (hence mark on forehead) and actions (mark on hand).

Rapture vs Second Coming

Aspect	Rapture	Second Coming (Revelation 19)
Jesus' location	Meets believers in the air (**1 Thessalonians 4:17**).	Comes to earth (**Revelation 19:11–21**).
Purpose	To gather the saints (kept from wrath)	To judge and rule those still on earth (destruction of enemies)
Audience	Believers only	All the world sees (**Revelation 1:7; Matthew 24:30**).
Timing	**Matthew 24:22** *"Tribulation of those days cut short"*: Before God's wrath	After the tribulation and before God's wrath
Result	Saints go to heaven	Jesus sets up His kingdom on earth (**Revelation 20**).

What is the Scroll as mentioned in Revelation 5?

The Scroll cannot be opened until all 7 seals are removed.

The contents of the scroll are God's end-time plan for the Earth:

- Judgment of the wicked - **Revelation 11:18** and **Revelation 20:11-12**.

- Vindication of the saints - **Revelation 19:7-8** and **2 Thessalonians 1:6-7**.

- Restoration of creation - **Revelation 21:1-5** and **Romans 8:19-22**.

- Transfer of rulership to Christ from the "*prince of this world*" - **Revelation 11:15**, **John 12:31**, and **Revelation 20:4**.

In effect, the scroll is a legal document, much like a title deed that an owner holds.

What Happens After Rapture

First, the 144,000 are sealed (**Revelation 7**) as witnesses to the coming wrath of God.

The 7 Trumpets

Trumpet 1 - **Revelation 8:7** - Hail, fire burns up 1/3 of the trees and grass

Trumpet 2 - **Revelation 8:8** - 1/3 sea turns to blood; sea life and ships destroyed

Trumpet 3 - **Revelation 8:10** - Star (asteroid?) "wormwood" falls on rivers and springs. 1/3 of the water is poisoned

Trumpet 4 - **Revelation 8:12** - Sun, moon, and stars darkened, lose 1/3 of their light

Trumpet 5 - **Revelation 9:1** - Star hits earth, opens pit - demonic locusts torment unbelievers for 5 months (**Revelation 9:5**)

Trumpet 6 - **Revelation 9:13** - 4 angels released. 1/3 of mankind killed, fire, smoke, and brimstone.

Between Trumpet 6 and Trumpet 7:
- The Two Witnesses (**Revelation 11:1-6**) prophesy for 42 months.
- The two witnesses are killed (**Revelation 11:7-10**).
- After 3.5 days, God resurrects the two witnesses (**Revelation 11:11**) and then they ascend to heaven, witnessed by their enemies (**Revelation 11:12**)
- A mighty earthquake kills 7000 in the same hour of their ascension (**Revelation 11:13**).

Trumpet 7 - **Revelation 11:15** Lightning, thunder, earthquake, great hail.

The 7 Bowl Judgements

Bowl 1 - **Revelation 16:2** - Physical sores on those with the mark of the beast

Bowl 2 - **Revelation 16:3** - Sea turns to blood, every living creature in the sea dies

Bowl 3 - **Revelation 16:4** - Rivers & springs turn to blood

Bowl 4 - **Revelation 16:8** - Sun becomes so hot it scorches the earth. Men still blaspheme God.

Bowl 5 - **Revelation 16:10** - Darkness

Bowl 6 - **Revelation 16:12** - Euphrates dries up. Unclean spirits come out of the mouth of the beast & the false prophet: they gather the kings of the earth to prepare for battle.

Bowl 7 - **Revelation 16:18-21** - Almighty earthquake, islands disappear, mountains disappear, great hail from heaven.

The Battle at Armageddon (the Greek word used is **Harmagedōn** which refers to the Mount of Megiddo, which is a strategic hill in northern Israel that overlooks the Jezreel Valley, a historical battleground). Refer **Revelation 16:16**: *"And they gathered them together to the place called in Hebrew, Armageddon."*

Revelation 19:11-21 - 2nd coming of Christ to deal the *"wrath of Almighty God"*.

Revelation 20:1-3 - Jesus wins; Satan is bound for 1000 years.

Revelation 20:5 - *"The rest of the dead did not live again until the thousand years were finished."*

Summary

Within this study I have endeavored to show what is, and what is not, scriptural when it comes to the rapture. I do believe, in discussions with various Christians regarding their own end times interpretation, that some who claim they are Mid-Trib or Post-Trib are essentially arguing for a Pre-Wrath position without realizing it, because they don't realize these two key end times distinctions are two separate eschatological phases;

- Tribulation (**thlipsis**) refers to suffering, persecution, and testing, including at the hands of the Antichrist, after the midpoint (**Matthew 24:21, Revelation 6:9-11**).
- Wrath (**orgē**) is God's righteous judgment on the wicked, which believers are promised to be exempt from (**1 Thessalonians 5:9**).

We can conclude, when we are inclusive of all verses pertaining to end times events, that 'imminent rapture' is a false teaching, and will leave many Christians who believe this doctrine to be severely unprepared to survive a great tribulation, both mentally and physically, if their belief that Christians will not see the great tribulation does not come to fruition.

I started out this study explaining that I had naively followed the 'teaching' of a pre-tribulation rapture. I concluded that this was the second most inaccurate view to hold, and that an 'after tribulation but before God's wrath' view was what the scripture was actually pointing to.

After more than 13 years of study, I came to the conclusion that the timing of the rapture was 'post trials, after great tribulation, before God's wrath'. Not a very catchy description, but one that reflects what the scripture actually states. It wasn't until 2025 that I started to receive feedback on my book, and my point of view was closely aligned with the 'Pre-Wrath' interpretation.

With the global 'pandemic' in 2020 and subsequent mandates related to mRNA 'vaccines', we saw that many Christians felt they were forced to take the injections, despite evidence it contained a DNA modifying spike protein, a substance called luciferase as admitted by court-ordered documents, and was created using aborted fetal cell lines, both in the testing and production of the 'vaccines'. Even though not one person was physically forced to receive the injections, the global event showed that many Christians complied to save their jobs and worldly possessions. The Vatican and many pastors stated that receiving the injections was morally acceptable due to the "lack of direct involvement in abortion". Pope Francis, Congregation for the Doctrine of the Faith (CDF), issued this statement on December 21, 2020.

How much more likely will unprepared Christians be to take the mark of the beast to buy (food) and sell (their time in return for wages).

So be Berean with everything you hear being preached and taught. And know that what you fill your life with will reflect who you are and what you believe. **1 Corinthians 3:16-17** says *"Do you not know that you are the temple of God and that the Spirit of God dwells in you? If anyone defiles the temple of God, God will destroy him. For the temple of God is holy, which temple you are."*

FAQ Part 1

These are my best guess answers, based on logic and discernment; I have provided scripture where possible. These are questions commonly asked; however, I have made the decision not to include these in the main part of my study.

Q01. Has the abomination of desolation begun globally in the early 2020s?

Answer: The answer is no - the Antichrist is a man; **Daniel 7:24-25** - Speaks of a king who will arise and "*speak great words against the Most High*", indicating a singular ruler.
2 Thessalonians 2:3-4 Refers to him as the "*man of sin*" and "*son of perdition*," who will sit in the temple of God, showing himself as God. The temple has not been rebuilt as of time of publishing.
Revelation 13:5-8 says that The Beast (Antichrist) is given a mouth to speak great things and blasphemies, and he will rule over the nations. **Revelation 19:20** - The Beast and the False Prophet are thrown alive into the lake of fire, indicating they are individuals.

Q02. How far off the End Times/ final week are we?

Answer: That is a question that no person living today has any clue about. Yes, things appear to be escalating quickly with events in Israel and the church, and sin is readily accepted in the name of tolerance; it is easy to assume that the end is near. We don't know exactly how long until Daniel's 70th week begins - only God does. But we see the pieces falling into place: Israel restored, peace agreements forming, temple preparations well underway (see https://templeinstitute.org/), power shifts and trade routes happening around the globe. That tells us the final week could be very soon, maybe even in our lifetime. The key is not guessing a date, but being ready, watchful, and faithful. We are told to look for the signs but not become consumed by distractions.

Q03. Will the rapture be a physical disappearance of bodies?

Answer: Considering that we will be given new bodies, (**1 Corinthians 15:51–53**) *"Behold, I shew you a mystery; We shall not all sleep, but we shall all be changed, In a moment, in the twinkling of an eye, at the last trump: for the trumpet shall sound, and the dead shall be raised incorruptible, and we shall be changed. For this corruptible must put on incorruption, and this mortal must put on immortality."* I doubt that our existing bodies will be taken with us. I don't believe that those who are 'dead in Christ' (**1 Thessalonians 4:16-17**) will reform from dust and ash. I could imagine that the movie 'Left Behind' (which is a pre-tribulation interpretation of the rapture), whereby physical bodies disappear, and clothes are neatly folded on the ground, is far from the truth. However, in contrast to this, imagine the mainstream media lies that would circulate if millions of people were to, in their eyes, 'suddenly drop dead' because their souls were taken to meet Jesus. People would, as the Bible states, be eating and drinking and giving in marriage up until the day of the Lord (**Matthew 24:37-39**). The Bible is not clear as to what will happen physically to the bodies of Christians at the moment of rapture, and to be honest, this is not an important aspect of our salvation. What is important is not to be fooled by a misinterpretation of the rapture, and to understand what prophesied events must take place prior to the rapture.

Q04. Who is the antichrist? Who/ what is the beast?

Answer: Regarding the antichrist: There are many things in this world that are not of God. If something is not of God and is against Christ, it is anti-Christ. The Bible confirms this in **1 John 2:18** *"even now many antichrists have come."* **1 John 2:22** says, *"whoever denies that Jesus is the Christ. Such a person is the antichrist - denying the Father and the Son."* It is important to be aware of and challenge anything that doesn't feel right. However, it is more important not to lose focus by actively seeking out 'what could be' the antichrist or the beast. People have speculated for 2,000 years about who the antichrist is or could be. This is ultimately a distraction. The sign we need to watch for is the man who makes a covenant with Israel for 7 years, likely to be centered around some form of peace agreement. I believe this points to a man, one who is admired and influential, possibly a peacemaker with instant impact.

Answer: Regarding the beast: Many people have speculated that the beast could be an economic or political system, or that it could be a false religion such as Catholicism (Rome is famously known as the city that sits on 7 hills). However, my suggestion is that the beast could be a global system that combines 3 strengths of unifying the world;
1. Economically (**Revelation 13:16-17** describes the mark that is required to buy and sell),
2. Politically (**Revelation 17:12-13** says the 10 horns are 10 kings who will give their power and authority to the beast, which is why so many thought that the mandated mRNA vaccinations was the mark of the beast, having been mandated by so many of the world's 'kings'), and
3. Some form of religious belief that is embraced on a massive scale - possibly climate fanaticism. **Revelation 13:11-15** tells us that the false prophet leads people into worship of the beast.

Q05. Some pastors teach that no Christians will suffer during the end times. Is this true?

Answer: Every time I hear this, I am absolutely disgusted at the audacity of this lie and the disrespect shown to millions of believers who have been killed for their faith in the last 2000 years and counting. Yes, Christians will experience great tribulation, as declared in **Revelation 6:7-8,** at the opening of the 4th seal.
In 2020, one Christian was killed about every 2 hours. In 2025 – over 7000 Christians have died in Nigeria alone. In just 5 years the persecution of Christians has doubled, resulting in a Christian being martyred every hour.

Yes, Christians will continue to die for their faith and beliefs as explicitly stated in **Revelation 20:4**: *"And I saw the souls of those who had been beheaded because of their testimony about Jesus and because of the word of God. They had not worshiped the beast or its image <u>and had not received its mark on their foreheads or their hands</u>. They came to life and reigned with Christ a thousand years."*

Q06. Are the Abrahamic Accords the covenant that Daniel and Revelation speak of?

Answer: No, I don't believe that the Abrahamic Accords themselves are the **Daniel 9:27** covenant, however they may be a foreshadowing that a future world leader could "confirm" with Israel and turn into that 7-year peace agreement as biblical prophecy states.

Q07. When did each rapture viewpoint begin?

Answer: Pre-Tribulation: Made popular by John Darby in 1930. It is the leading 21st-century viewpoint.

Answer: Mid-Tribulation: Developed by Norman B. Harrison and gained popularity in the early 1950s as it highlighted many omissions and contradictions within the very popular pre-tribulation theory.

Answer: Post-Tribulation: The post-tribulation view is historically rooted back to the early church, but the formal term itself – 'post-tribulation' - is a product of 20th-century theological categorization of end times events.

Answer: Pre-Wrath: the phrase was coined in 1990 by Marvin Rosenthal to accurately describe when the Bible stated that the rapture was to occur. It outlines that many prophesied events must occur before the rapture.

Q08. Why is Pre-Tribulation teaching so popular?

Answer: For the first 1800 years of church history, there was no pre- or post-tribulation teaching that focused on rapture. Believers generally expected persecution before Christ's return (which is post-tribulation or pre-wrath).

Pre-tribulation became a dominant viewpoint because it is emotionally attractive - it promises an escape from any form of persecution. It fits in with a Western Christian mindset that teaches prosperity, comfort, safety, and blessing - the focus of entertainment-style churches. This 'prosperity gospel' teaches that 'God wants you happy, not suffering.'

Mass Media and Pop culture have had a massive impact on spreading their message - 'The Late Great Planet Earth' (1970) sold millions of copies; the 'Left Behind' novels and movies starred Hollywood actors. Christian TV, radio, podcasts, and prophecy conferences almost always lean towards pre-tribulation.

Bible colleges and seminaries in the USA adopted dispensational theology, resulting in pastors who are trained under these systems rarely hearing of alternative teachings.

Congregations readily and easily accept the teaching because they lack the Berean mindset and *"examined the Scriptures every day to see if what Paul said was true"* (**Acts 17:11**) and simply trust what their pastor says. Adding to the Sunday-Christian mindset, they never dig deeper into anything more than a verse.

Pre-tribulation is also the nicest and neatest theory when it comes to presenting in a chart: Rapture, Tribulation, Millennium, Eternity. However, for the teachers of this theory to attain this, they cherry-pick scriptures, and they do it out of chronological order.

Q09. Can you take the Mark of the Beast and still be saved?

Answer: This is an incredibly dangerous statement and one that was made by Pastor John MacArthur. It completely contradicts what the Bible says in **Revelation 14:9-10**. MacArthur said this on September 24, 1980, at a Bible Questions and Answers Q&A session. He needs this statement to be true because MacArthur was a pre-tribulation preacher right up to the time of his death in July 2025 - he needed there to be, what he called, 'tribulation saints' even though there is no such mention of this term anywhere in the Bible. He explained that if people became saved after the tribulation began (because the rapture had already taken place before tribulation and therefore before the mark of the beast), they would be granted God's grace for taking the mark of the beast and be saved. The Bible would state this if this were the case, but it says the opposite in **Revelation 14**. MacArthur believed and taught pre-tribulation theology and believed that the seals are a part of God's wrath.

FAQ Part 2

Preparing for the future: scripture shows us several people who were instructed to prepare for what was to come. This was faith-based preparation - they prepared in obedience, not panic.

Joseph was instructed through divine revelation by interpreting Pharoh's dream to prepare, and the preparation was for a specific period: seven years of storage to survive seven years of famine.

Noah spent over 100 years preparing for the flood.

Hezekiah was told to prepare water for the city of Jerusalem for a period of siege (**2 Chronicles 32:2-4, 2 Chronicles 32:30**).

"A prudent man foresees evil and hides himself, but the simple pass on and are punished." (**Proverbs 22:3**).

Q10. Why does the Bible say 'run for the hills'? (Matthew 24:15)

Answer: The Bible actually states to leave Judea, because the antichrist will be seated in the rebuilt temple in Jerusalem. However, we know that persecution will be on a global scale. Sudden lockdowns and forced worship of the beast/ antichrist could be similar to those in Daniel's time, or with recent global lockdowns of 2020. Possibly, the 'mark of the beast' could be so suddenly introduced that you cannot buy and sell or travel within a 24-hour period. This is 100% possible if a sudden global internet blackout or an orchestrated global bank system 'collapse' were to occur.

Q11. How much time do I have to prepare once Seal 1 is opened?

Answer: To answer this, we should keep in mind that **Seal 2** is wars, and **Seal 3** is famine. With wars, commodities become more expensive. With famine, extreme shortages occur - so it may be too late to start storing away items then. If you feel you should put aside stores, you need time (and $) to prepare. Once the covenant is made by the antichrist, we may have weeks, months, or only a year to prepare - the Bible is not clear on a timeframe.

Q12. How long should your preparations last?

Answer: Daniel's 70th week lasts for 7 years, so no longer than 7 years. If the 2nd and 3rd seals make preparations more difficult, then you might decide somewhere between 3.5 and 7 years is required. Discernment tells me that the enforcement of the 'mark' will be around the time of the 2nd or 4th seal. We know that the 'Great Tribulation' begins at Seal 4, which occurs at the halfway mark of the 70th week, so in my opinion, you should assume at least 3.5 years of not being able to buy and sell in conventional methods.

Q13. What physically needs to be prepared for?

Answer: Not every group in history undergoing persecution has suffered, because they saw the impending signs and they acted. Take Jews in WW2, for example. So, my thoughts would be to make sure you have enough food stores, medical and market garden preparations to last out most of Daniel's 70th week.

Glossary of Terms

English / Theological Terms

Term	Definition
Antichrist	The end-time ruler who opposes Christ and persecutes Israel and the church.
Day of the Lord	A defined period of God's wrath beginning after the rapture.
Daniel's Seventieth Week	The final seven-year period decreed for Israel, culminating in the Day of the Lord.
God's Wrath	God's direct judgment poured out during the Day of the Lord through the trumpets and bowls.
Great Tribulation	Severe persecution of believers under Antichrist, distinct from God's wrath.
Kingdom of God	Christ's righteous rule, fully realised at His return and millennial reign.
Rapture	The catching away of believers to meet Christ before the outpouring of God's wrath.
Resurrection	The bodily raising of the dead by the power of God.
Seals	Preliminary judgments in Revelation that reveal events and conditions leading up to God's wrath, but are not themselves the outpouring of God's wrath.
Second Coming	The visible return of Jesus Christ to judge the world and establish His kingdom.
Trumpet Judgments	Judgments following the seventh seal, marking the beginning of God's wrath.

Term	Definition
Bowl Judgments	The final and intensified outpouring of God's wrath upon the earth.
Tribulation	Affliction and persecution experienced by believers, not an expression of God's wrath.
(Daniel's) 70th Week	The final seven-year period prophesied in Daniel 9:24-27, culminating in the Day of the Lord and the return of Christ.

The above terms are defined according to their biblical usage within this study, recognizing the distinction Scripture makes between tribulation endured by believers and the wrath of God poured out during the Day of the Lord.

The following terms are from the original language scripture was written in.

Hebrew Terms (Old Testament)

Term	Meaning
Shavuim	'sevens'
Gôy	Gentiles or Nations; non-Hebrew people.

Greek Terms (New Testament)

Term	Meaning
Apokalypsis	Revelation or unveiling.
Apostasia	Rebellion, deserter, falling away
Harpazō	To seize or catch away suddenly; permanent removal; translates to rapture.
Hápantas	Took them away
Parousia	Presence or coming; used of Christ's return.
Eschatos	Last
Thlipsis	Tribulation, pressure, or affliction.
Thymos	Wrath of God
Orgē	Wrath of God's furious anger.
Peirasmos	Trial, to test.
tēreō ek	Keep you
Pántas	'destroyed them all'
Ean mē	'Unless'

Scripture Reference Index by Topic/Keyword

Fulfilled & Future Prophesy

- **Zechariah 9:9** (Prophesy of Jesus 1st coming)
- **Matthew 21:1-11** (Prophesy fulfilled)
- **Daniel 9:20-27**
  - **9:26** (Messiah 'cut off')
  - **9:27** (City & sanctuary (temple) destroyed)
  - **9:27** (Abomination & end of sacrifice & offering)
- **Matthew 24:2** (Jesus prophesies temple destruction)

False Teachers & Leadership Warnings

- **Matthew 24:11** (False prophets)
- **2 Peter 2:1-3** (False teachers will exploit you)
- **Colossians 2:8** (Deceptive philosophy)
- **James 3:1** (Teachers judged more strictly)
- **Ezekiel 33:6** (Instruction to watchmen)
- **Matthew 18:6** (To those who cause others to stumble)
- **Acts 20:29-30** (Those you know will deceive)
- **Matthew 24:23-24,26** (Christians will be deceived)

Apostasy: Falling Away

- **2 Thessalonians 2:3** (Don't let anyone deceive you)
- **Colossians 2:8** (Warning of deceptive philosophy)
- **1 Timothy 4:1-2** (Christians follow deception)
- **Matthew 24:10-12** (Christians leaving the faith)
- **2 Timothy 4:3-4** (Many will follow false teachers)

Antichrist revealed

- **John 14:30** 'ruler of this world is coming'
- **2 Thessalonians 2:3** 'man of sin'
- **2 Thessalonians 2:4** (Sits as God in the temple of God)
- **Daniel 9:26-27** 'the prince who is to come'
- **Matthew 24:15** 'abomination, standing in the holy place'

Great Tribulation, Persecution

- **1 Thessalonians 3:3-4** (Expect tribulation and affliction)
- **Matthew 24:1-44** (Jesus tells disciples of His return)
- **Matthew 24:9-11** (Many will leave the faith)
- **Matthew 24:21-22** (Great tribulation at midpoint)
- **Daniel 9:27** (Covenant for 7 years broken at midpoint)
- **Revelation 6:1-8** (Seals 1 to 4)
- **Revelation 6:9-11** (Seal 5, cry of the martyrs)
- **Revelation 13:5-8** (Beast wages war for 42 months)
- **Revelation 13:16** (Mark of the beast)

Signs & Celestial Disturbances

- **Daniel 9:27** (Covenant with 'prince')
- **Joel 2:30-31** (Celestial signs before 2nd coming)
- **Matthew 24:29** (Celestial signs)
- **Revelation 6:12-14** (Seal 6)
- **Luke 21:25-28** (Celestial signs then Son of Man)
- **Malachi 4:5** (Elijah returns before Day of Lord)

Rapture

- **1 Thessalonians 4:16-17** (*harpázō*)
- **Matthew 24:22** (Days cut short)
- **Matthew 24:30-31** (Elect are gathered globally)
- **Revelation 7:14** (Out of great tribulation)
- **John 14:3** (Jesus promise to take us)
- **Matthew 25:1-13** (Wise virgins)

Second Coming

- **Matthew 24:27** (All eyes will see Jesus return)
- **Luke 21:27-28** (Son of Man comes in a cloud)
- **Acts 1:9-11** (Jesus will return in manner He left)
- **Revelation 1:7** (Jesus comes in clouds, all eyes will see)
- **1 Thessalonians 4:17** (*harpázō* to clouds)
- **Luke 17:30** (Son of Man returns suddenly)

Day of the Lord

- **Obadiah 1:15** (Day of the Lord)
- **Isaiah 13:9-22** (Day of the Lord)
- **Zephaniah 1:2-18** (Day of the Lord)

Wrath of God

- **Revelation 8+9** (Seal 7 & the Trumpet Judgements)
- **2 Peter 3:10-12** (Destruction by fire)
- **Revelation 6:16-17** (Hiding in caves)
- **Revelation 16:1** (7 bowls of Gods wrath)
- **Revelation 16:2-21** (Bowl by bowl)
- **Revelation 14:9-10** (Those with mark of beast)
- **Revelation 19:15** (Fury of wrath of God)
- **1 Thessalonians 5:9** (Christians won't suffer wrath)
- **Romans 5:9** (We are saved from God's wrath)

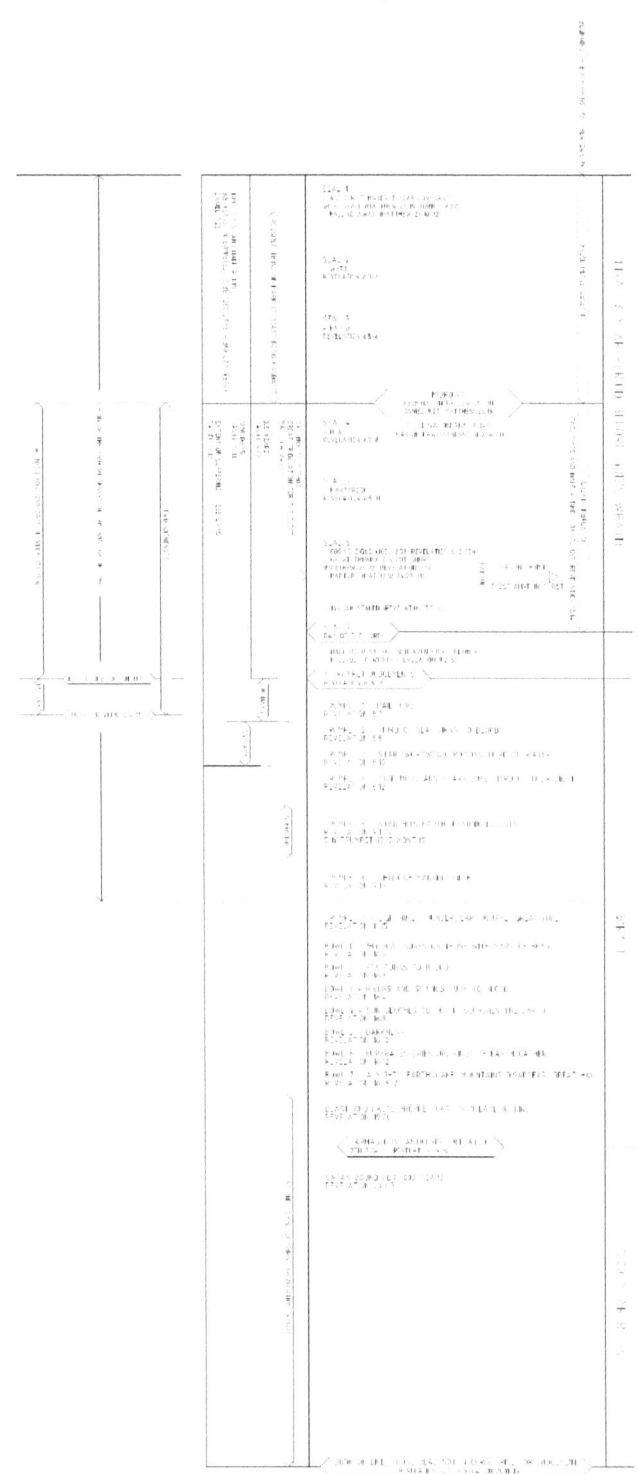

End Times Truth and Lies
Biblical Evidence

Few topics in the church stir more debate than the end times. Is the rapture pre-tribulation, mid-tribulation, or post-tribulation?

What is the difference between tribulation and wrath?

Which view is truly biblical?

In **Eschatology Truth and Lies: A Biblical Study**, the Scriptures are examined with clarity and precision, exposing common misconceptions and presenting a compelling case for the Pre-Wrath view. This study challenges tradition by returning to the authority of God's Word - fact, not opinion - so believers can face the future with confidence and hope.

www.ingramcontent.com/pod-product-compliance
Lightning Source LLC
Chambersburg PA
CBHW071636040426
42452CB00009B/1651